A Legacy for Maine

THE NOVEMBER COLLECTION OF

Elizabeth B. Noyce

Martha
Merry Christmas.
David
1997

JESSICA F. NICOLL

PORTLAND MUSEUM OF ART
1997

ROCKWELL KENT
Maine Coast

circa 1907

oil on canvas

28 1/8 x 38 in.

Farnsworth Art Museum

The vision that Elizabeth B. Noyce pursued in building her superb collection was driven by her intellectual vitality and independence. The influence of others was rarely a force in her aesthetic decision making. At the same time, Betty's quest to discover and return to Maine the finest examples of painting created in her state was an exceptionally unselfish act. Her ultimate goal was the creation of a rich resource for her neighbors—which is to say for the people of Maine.

This catalog and exhibition strive to convey the spirited nature of Betty's approach to collecting and the elegance of her judgment. To record the history of Betty's extraordinary collection necessitated the collaboration of six Maine institutions—the Portland Museum of Art, the Farnsworth Art Museum, the Monhegan Museum, the Maine Maritime Academy, the Maine State Museum, and the Maine Maritime Museum—and the crucial assistance of the Noyce family. The result is a heartfelt tribute to an unforgettable woman and her unique generosity to Maine.

The three sponsors of this exhibition—Maine Bank & Trust, the John J. Nissen Baking Company, and the law firm of Perkins, Thompson, Hinckley & Keddy—represent an alliance of the three corporations that empowered Betty's dreams for a growing and vibrant Maine economy. The three essays in this catalog—by friend and advisor Owen Wells, by Farnsworth Art Museum Chief Curator Susan Larsen, and by Portland Museum of Art Chief Curator Jessica Nicoll—reveal how effectively Betty combined corporate dynamics with philanthropy and how gracefully she moved between these two worlds.

The hundreds of people who were her friends—and the thousands who appreciated and admired her—can no longer experience the often enigmatic and always memorable pleasure of her presence. This celebration of her role as collector allows us the opportunity to revisit her own personal world: her vision of excellence, her preference for essential truth, her taste for unspoiled landscape and unflawed humanity.

The enduring impact of Elizabeth B. Noyce's affection for Maine extends far beyond the visual arts and the elegant works recorded in this publication. Betty's commitment to art was equaled or exceeded by her devotion to issues of public education, health, and economic benefit. By sharing her great collection with her chosen state we wish to honor the many dimensions of her love for Maine.

Daniel E. O'Leary
Director
Portland Museum of Art

Christopher P. Crosman
Director
Farnsworth Art Museum

One of Elizabeth Noyce's greatest gifts was her ability to set up situations that brought people together to work creatively and constructively toward common goals. The insight that collaboration is key to building and sustaining community drove all of her philanthropies. This catalogue and the exhibition it accompanies, organized in Mrs. Noyce's honor and dedicated to her memory, represent one more fulfillment of her vision of the people and institutions of Maine working in concord.

The purpose of *A Legacy for Maine* has been to document and commemorate the November Collection that Elizabeth Noyce created and gave to the people of Maine. This goal could not have been achieved without the generous assistance of the many individuals and organizations that are part of this story. At the head of this list is Owen Wells, whose support, knowledge, and encouragement have kept this project on course. I am deeply indebted to the Noyce family for their crucial participation, and to Tom Cattell who aided my efforts to record the full scope and history of the November Collection.

This catalogue and the exhibition it accompanies could not have been accomplished without the partnership of the Farnsworth Art Museum, and I appreciate the help that Christopher Crosman, Susan Larsen, Pamela Belanger, and Edith Murphy gave in the midst of many other pressing demands. I would also like to thank colleagues from throughout the state who joined in this effort, including Ed Deci, Monhegan Museum; Rand Erb, Maine Maritime Academy; Julia Hunter, Maine State Museum; and Robert Webb, Maine Maritime Museum. Helpful information about the origins and contents of the November Collection was furnished by independent fine art dealers Terry Geaghan and Geoff Robinson, Tom Crotty of the Frost Gully Gallery, Peter Rathbone and Dara Mitchell of Sotheby's, Peter Ralston, and John Wilmerding.

Elizabeth Wiley served as the research assistant for this project, providing invaluable support both as a sleuth and a sounding board. I am grateful to Henry Brooks, Tom Myron, Owen Wells, Katherine and Roger Woodman, and my colleagues at the Portland Museum of Art for reading the catalogue and improving its factual and grammatical accuracy, and to Susan Ransom for her thorough editing. Thanks are also due to Michael Mahan and his staff for designing a publication in harmony with the grace, beauty, and gusto of the collection it portrays.

I would like to thank the Board of Trustees and Daniel O'Leary, Director, of the Portland Museum of Art for entrusting me with this project. And finally, acknowledgment is due to Perkins, Thompson, Hinckley & Keddy, Maine Bank & Trust Company, and the John J. Nissen Baking Company who provided the very generous support that made *A Legacy for Maine* possible.

Jessica F. Nicoll
Chief Curator
Portland Museum of Art

FREDERICK CHILDE HASSAM

Isles of Shoals

1915

oil on canvas

25 x 30 in.

Portland Museum of Art

OWEN W. WELLS

Introduction

It could be said that Maine art is its own genre. Many of Maine's artists have focused upon and captured the state's unique synergy of beauty and severity. Depictions of welcoming harbors and serene coastal villages often bear subtle tinges of hardship or resistance, whether in the form of ominous cloud cover, or the concentrated grimace of an aged fisherman. The austerity of Maine's landscape is tempered, and occasionally beautified, by the perseverance of its communities. In many ways, Maine and its art represent the importance of community in man's struggle to live and function in a constantly challenging environment. It is this victorious spirit of community, as unique to Maine as its forbidding coast, that drew Elizabeth ("Betty") Noyce to Maine, and ultimately to its art.

Betty grew up in Auburn, Massachusetts, the daughter of a blue-collar worker. After marrying Robert Noyce, she reluctantly left New England and moved first to Philadelphia and then to California to accommodate her husband's ambitious career. In California, Betty's love of art remained relatively dormant, but for occasional flashes of artistic passion expressed through her participation in her children's crafts projects or the assembly of Halloween costumes. For nearly twenty years, Betty tolerated the turbulent, fast-paced California lifestyle, suppressing her artistic inclinations and her insuperable longing to return to New England. Back then, summer was Betty's salvation; the annual pilgrimage to Maine fortified her weakened spirit, always, however, bringing tears when it came time to return to California.

After her divorce, Betty left California with decided urgency and returned to Maine for good. In time, the real "Betty" re-emerged. As her daughter Pendred reflects, "Maine healed her." As Betty came to identify Maine as her true home, her spirit flourished. Shedding the superfluities of California, Betty basked in the simplicity of a "common" Maine life. As her friend Marcia Chapman recalls, she "could be invisible here and could go and work the rummage sale and there was no big deal. She was just a neighbor." In her element, Betty would drive herself around the small town of Bremen in an Oldsmobile; she would frequent Moody's Diner, where she would stand in line with the other patrons, waiting for a green vinyl booth to become available and for a waitress to bellow unreflectively "Betty!" in the same tone she used to call for meatloaf. She would gather with friends and neighbors at the Muscongus Community Center for weekly sauerkraut suppers and bridge games; and she would make crafts and sew quilts for community events. Betty's spirit resided where things and people were real.

Coming home to Maine also revitalized Betty's appreciation for art. In 1983, Betty involved herself in the construction of the new Portland Museum of Art, serving on the Public Relations Committee. She took particular delight in organizing events for the national press which was brought to Maine to showcase the Museum and the opening. In the hotel room of each media representative, she left a basket of Maine products filled with fresh apples, canned blueberries, maple syrup, and lobster knick-knacks. The media never knew that this was not standard fare for hotel guests, but they loved it and wrote glowingly about the new building.

It was through our mutual involvement with the Museum that I came to know Betty; in time, I became her attorney, personal advisor, and friend. Our personalities and perspectives seemed to complement each other, and together we embarked upon the hugely satisfying task of developing and implementing her many philanthropic ideas. Betty and I also worked together on her art collection, frequently discussing various artists and identifying suitable works of art to purchase. While I knew little about Maine art and the artists who painted here, Betty submerged herself in the subject, acquiring and devouring hundreds of art books. Experts such as Tom Crotty, Terry Geaghan, and Geoff Robinson; Museum Directors Daniel O'Leary and Christopher Crosman; Curator Jessica Nicoll; and Sotheby's American art authorities Peter Rathbone and Dara Mitchell all helped to mold Betty's collection.

In time, Betty became a trustee of both the Portland Museum of Art and the Farnsworth Art Museum. Through her involvement with the museums, Betty also came to know Andrew and Jamie Wyeth, an event which inspired Betty's early acquisition of N. C. Wyeth's *Dark Harbor Fishermen* (cover), her favorite work of art, which she displayed in her dining room for the remainder of her life.

On a visit with the Wyeths at Broad Cove Farm, I learned that the owner of *Dark Harbor Fishermen* wished to sell the work. I knew immediately that Betty would be captivated by it . . . and she was. In large measure, *Dark Harbor Fishermen* represented for Betty all that she loved about Maine—the sea, the haunting self-sufficiency of Maine people, and the perfect blend of man with nature.

Elizabeth Noyce at her home

Betty's relationship with Andrew and Jamie Wyeth continued, and her affection for them and her love of their work resulted in her acquisition of *Maine Room* (p.10), *Coast Guard Anchor* (p.14), *Irises at Sea*, and several others.

Betty's renewed interest in art prompted frequent trips to Sotheby's in New York, an experience which she dreaded but for the excitement of the quest in search of art works depicting Maine. From New York, home to Maine, came the wonderful Fitz Hugh Lane, *Camden Mountains from the South Entrance to the Harbor* (p.63), the John Marin, *Boat Fantasy, Deer Isle, Maine, No. 30* (p.11), which had been in the collection of photographer and Marin friend, Alfred Stieglitz, and the Edward Hopper, *Railroad Crossing, Rockland, Maine*. For Betty, art was more than an investment, it was an experience.

ANDREW WYETH
Maine Room

1991

watercolor and graphite on paper

28 1/4 x 36 1/4 in.

Portland Museum of Art

JOHN MARIN
Boat Fantasy, Deer Isle, Maine, No. 30

1928

watercolor and crayon on paper

18 x 23 1/8 in.

Portland Museum of Art

Most of Betty's collecting came in the last seven to eight years of her life. In a sense, the November Collection is a culmination of her appreciation for Maine, and the knowledge and sophistication acquired along the way. For Betty, it was the process of collecting—the people she met, the places she visited, and the sense of history she attained—more than the actual acquisition of the paintings that fueled her fire. Betty seemed more affected by the spirit of the painter than by the physical representation of the painting itself. Her appreciation resided at the level of artistic motivation; the paintings themselves served as invitations to seek out and experience the sources of the artists' inspirations. In that sense, Betty was more of an artist than a collector. Betty would rather board her boat *Tumblehome* and travel to the Isles of Shoals to experience firsthand the vision that had inspired Childe Hassam than attend a show exhibiting the products of those scenes and inspirations. Climbing the rocks with her friends, Katherine Woodman, Rachel Armstrong, and Jessica Nicoll, Betty delighted in seeing the same craggy outcroppings that Hassam had seen in 1915 when he completed *Isles of Shoals* (p.6).

Intrigued by Fitz Hugh Lane's annual cruises through the Penobscot Bay region, Betty discovered the Luminist movement of the mid-nineteenth century and added *Castine Harbor* (p.22) to her collection. In Eastman Johnson's work, Betty found the unassuming beauty of country life; with Winslow Homer, she saw the raw beauty of coastal life. In the work of Childe Hassam and Charles Woodbury, Betty viewed Maine through the eyes of the Impressionists; through Gertrude Fiske, Woodbury's pupil, she discovered the inspiration for the Modernist movement in Maine; and through the works of Robert Henri, Rockwell Kent, George Bellows, Leon Kroll, and John Marin, portraying the regions of Maine that she called "home," Betty felt a tremendous sense of security and belonging. In time, a historical structure and an independent identity for Maine art emerged in Betty's mind, and the November Collection was born.

While the collection asserts itself as perhaps the most impressive array of Maine art ever assembled by an individual, until recently the spirit of its origination had remained shrouded in the humble and protective deference of anonymity. Creative speculation may contrive romantic explanations for the origin of "November Collection," a name that served to preserve the anonymity Betty treasured, but in fact, its inspiration was purely whimsical. Betty had a penchant for whimsicality: in 1989, Betty needed a name for a charitable foundation she had established; thinking of her October birthdate, Betty called it the "Libra Foundation." When it came time to assign a name to a corporation formed to own some of her real estate, she called it "October Corporation." Another corporation, established for other business ventures, was named "August Corporation." When asked to exhibit her burgeoning art collection, she sought to conceal its ownership with a name, and chose "November Collection"... because she liked the sound of it.

The November Collection, while extremely inclusive, does not pretend to be comprehensive, and some would accurately observe that it has large gaps when viewed as a landscape of Maine painting. The collection traces the evolution of Maine art as appreciated by Betty Noyce. It was not Betty's intention to assemble a complete collection of Maine art; she merely collected what she liked. The extent to which the November Collection embodies the history of Maine art is incidental, and solely attributable to the depth and breadth of Betty's appreciation for Maine. Through her generosity and vision, the collection will be nurtured in the custody of Maine's wonderful public museums, the Portland Museum of Art, the Farnsworth Art Museum, the Maine Maritime Museum, the Maine State Museum, and the Monhegan Museum. Betty's legacy is an experience called "Maine."

JAMIE WYETH
Coast Guard Anchor

1982

watercolor on paper

22 x 30 1/4 in.

Farnsworth Art Museum

SUSAN C. LARSEN

Twice a Gift

Collecting art is a private adventure that has important consequences for the public realm of art. Collectors are generally the first patrons of living artists and play a role in the aesthetic and social temperament of artistic movements and cultural communities. Collectors often describe early and emotional attachments to a favorite artistic style, to personally relevant subject matter, or to the individual expression of an artist. Upon reflection, collectors frequently recall that they first responded to a strong feeling that their lives might be enhanced by spending time in the company of beautiful or provocative works of art. Seemingly random acquisitions begin to coalesce into an environment of objects with a certain character. Sometimes a collection will reveal elements or aspirations of the collector's own nature. Classic and reassuring, innovative and disturbing, composed of historical masterworks or made up of risky, cutting-edge choices, every collection is utterly unique, conceived within the understanding and temperament of a person over a given period of time. Its existence as an ensemble is, alas, temporary but its having existed is crucial to the destiny of public institutions.

A traditional lesson within the art historian's curriculum is the concept that works of art frequently, if not always, return to the community in which they were made. We can immediately think of Italian Renaissance masterpieces in British or French state collections and of French Impressionist works cherished by the patrons of museums across the United States, but these are the notable exceptions to the norm. Most of us have also seen and understood that art has its roots in particular communities, practices, and places. Art dealers know that the best market for landscapes of almost any place is the very same environment in which they were made and among the people who know and love a region and its history.

Traveling in the United States or abroad, one discovers unusual depths and many wonderful surprises in individual museum collections devoted to the art of a home country, a region, a city. National and civic pride require that each country's historical voice speak prominently in its important museums. It is this inner dialogue conveyed through works of art that fascinates the art historian, the cultural anthropologist, and the social historian as well as the museum visitor. People look to the art of their area in hopes of finding their own cherished values affirmed and renewed by their forebears and contemporaries while understanding that these values may also be exposed and brought under scrutiny. Through art we are able to learn of people, events, traditions, and the many places and flavors of this world. We look to our cultural institutions to preserve and make public these vivid and eloquent objects so that continuity is assured and a rich, multi-layered cultural conversation may continue through generations.

When a work of art passes from private hands into the keeping of a public institution, it becomes part of the cultural inheritance of an entire community of citizens, present and future. Generations of museum-goers grow up in the company of a work of art, grow used to seeing it and having it available for their reflection and enjoyment and, in turn, offer it as a gift to their own children, who will continue this special relationship. When a major work of art speaks to the history and spirit of a place it is suddenly available to many eyes and minds who will take from it and bring to it new life experiences relevant to the present and reflective of the content the artist wished to preserve and impart.

Among important American collectors of our own time, Elizabeth B. Noyce was an unusual person. Her delight in living with works of art was genuine and hearty even while her sense of their intended place within the community was clear. Choosing to collect the art of Maine, she soon focused her activity. In doing so, she understood a first principle in the creation of a distinguished collection, which requires a sense of purpose, a bit of self-discipline, and a more or less clearly envisioned goal. The pleasure principle was also evidently honored in the collecting life of Elizabeth Noyce. Her choices are alive with color, full of figures doing interesting, difficult, and important things. Maine's people are everywhere in this collection: building ships, hauling fish from stout vessels, laboring in the canneries, tending their children, even eyeing the "summer folk," who are also part of this wonderfully inclusive human picture of the state, past and present. Landscape images have a specificity, a great deal of information and mood to impart even as they are resplendently evocative of the breadth, wildness, indeed the natural allure of Maine. One senses that her acquisitions were twice a gift: to herself for as long as she might have them; simultaneously a gift to the citizens of her beloved state.

Works of art within the collection are overwhelmingly figurative, and there is little to indicate her interest in the more hermetic, theoretical questions of contemporary art criticism. In an interesting way, Elizabeth Noyce often seemed to choose the work of artists whose vision ranged beyond the narrow confines of their own private psychology, who cared about the greater human community and said so through their imagery, content, and style. Hers was an affirmative vision, which she honored in the art selected for the collection. Scenes depicted emphasize the capable, generous, hard-working character of a people used to tasks involving cooperation and intricate craftsmanship. They are imbued with a spirit of good fellowship in the workplace and pride in the effort of a group doing traditional tasks together. These paintings invite us to discover just how and why people were engaged with the land, the sea, and each other. It is clear that Elizabeth Noyce saw a great deal of continuity between Maine's industries past and present.

Collections, even if they are privately held, are generally created with an intended audience in mind. Some collectors seek to assemble a group of impressive masterworks for their own enjoyment and as evidence of personal status and

GEORGE BELLOWS
The Teamster

1916

oil on canvas

34 x 44 in.

Farnsworth Art Museum

EDWARD HOPPER
Lime Rock Quarry No. 1

1926

watercolor on paper

14 x 20 in.

Farnsworth Art Museum

consummate connoisseurship. Other collectors pursue a category of art objects wishing to fill an envisioned set of known and related works, almost in the manner of a stamp collector. Collectors of contemporary art often follow a series of fashionable artists and movements in the art world, constantly changing and churning the collection to stay apace with current taste. Rare and wonderful are those collections which alter the history of art or the history of taste through new insight into a period or a group of artists by assembling a visual spectacle so convincing and marvelous that it sweeps aside conventional wisdom.

Elizabeth Noyce's love of art, it would seem, has much to do with her great understanding of life and people and her desire to share the most positive and supportive aspects of Maine's recent past with subsequent generations. One by one, her paintings by Fitz Hugh Lane, Winslow Homer, Eastman Johnson, John Marin, Edward Hopper, N. C. Wyeth, Andrew Wyeth, Emily Muir, William Muir, and so many others bring their best insights about Maine to life for us all. They tell us of daily experiences in home and work and affirm our private moments of transcendence when we suddenly grasp the deep beauty of this place. Art and life never lose their direct connection in the collection of Elizabeth Noyce. Each work communicates clearly and positively to an audience capable of seeing and understanding artistic subtleties but also to those, especially young people, who are just learning to do so. In a museum setting, as at home, learning is ideally motivated by a promise and fulfillment of enjoyment and personal growth. One can see and sense how Elizabeth Noyce grew to understand the intangible but real difference between fine works of art and truly great ones. She made room for a broad spectrum of artists and styles but did not fail to secure major masterworks when such opportunities arose. These have provided the essential shape and underpinnings of her important collection.

Just a short time ago, the Portland Museum of Art and the Farnsworth Art Museum collaborated on the exhibition *A Brush with Greatness*, featuring a selection of American watercolors from the collection of Elizabeth Noyce. The title had, we sadly realized, a double meaning when we learned of her untimely passing. It was a very telling and appropriate phrase because it focused our attention upon her genuine ambition for the collection and now, by implication, for the citizens of Maine.

Elizabeth Noyce set a standard for the permanent collections of our institutions that has lifted our sights and challenged us to think as highly of Maine's past and future as she did. Hers was a seldom seen, rather noble, and almost old-fashioned concept of generosity. She did not merely give away the works she could spare, or those she had grown tired of, or those appropriate to one's present collection. Elizabeth Noyce provided our institutions with her best, which have become our best. In so doing, she has helped us to see not only who we are but what she wished for us and what we might become.

FITZ HUGH LANE
Castine Harbor

1852

oil on canvas

20 1/8 x 30 1/8 in.

Portland Museum of Art

JESSICA F. NICOLL

Private Vision—Public Purpose

Elizabeth Bottomley Noyce (1930-1996), familiarly and fondly known as "Betty," became legendary in her lifetime for her extraordinary generosity to the people and institutions of Maine, her adopted home. Through her broad-based support for causes ranging from healthcare to the preservation of Maine's islands and coast, she consistently acted on her belief that personal wealth was most usefully applied to communal well-being. Her culminating act of philanthropy was a bequest of more than 150 paintings and sculpture to museums of art and history throughout the state. These gifts revealed this resolutely private woman as an avid and astute collector who had assembled a group of artworks marked by excellence and expressive of her passions: Maine, the sea, the family, and the comforts of home. The November Collection, as Mrs. Noyce named it, bears the stamp of its creator, both in the subjects and styles it encompasses, and in its disposition. Instead of choosing to establish the collection in her name at one museum, she dispersed it among institutions throughout Maine–the Farnsworth Art Museum, Maine Maritime Academy, Maine Maritime Museum, Monhegan Museum, and Portland Museum of Art; in doing so, she placed public service above self-aggrandizement. Her gifts of art endow Maine's cultural institutions with a record of the remarkable history of art in the state and will make that history broadly available to the people of Maine for generations to come.

As the November Collection moves into the public realm from the private sphere in which it was created, there is an opportunity to document how it came into being and to explore what it reveals about a woman who left an indelible mark on the present and future of Maine. For much of the last two decades, Mrs. Noyce was publicly visible through her charitable gifts, estimated at more than 75 million dollars, to organizations ranging from the University of Maine to the Maine Medical Center. However, she rarely stepped into the spotlight her philanthropy afforded, choosing instead to live quietly on the coast of Maine, enjoying the company of family and friends and the pleasures of good books, puzzles, needlework, and boating. She became increasingly engaged in studying and collecting American art—particularly art with connections to Maine. The majority of the works she acquired were displayed in her two homes, and when they were lent to public exhibitions they were identified only as from the November Collection.[1] Consequently, few people were aware of her deep, personal interest in art or of the scope and quality of the collection she was forming.

Mrs. Noyce's activities as an art collector paralleled the evolution and focus of her philanthropy. Just as her giving was directed almost exclusively within Maine, first in her town and later throughout the state, so, too, her collecting focused primarily on Maine's artistic traditions. She began on a small scale in the 1970s, acquiring paintings, mostly in watercolor, by artists working in her immediate community. As her interest in Maine developed, she became a keen student of the state's rich and varied art history. Her ambitions as a collector expanded as her understanding of the breadth, beauty, and importance of that history deepened. In the end, she created a collection that included works by most of the major artists who have drawn inspiration from the state's provocative beauty.

The earliest works from the collection date to the arrival in Maine in the nineteenth century of the first American landscape painters, including Alvan Fisher, Fitz Hugh Lane, and Frederic Church. Mrs. Noyce's personal preferences were in concert with the dominant tradition of realism in Maine.

As the collection grew, it encompassed the evolution of that tradition with paintings by Winslow Homer, Robert Henri, Rockwell Kent, George Bellows, Edward Hopper, and three generations of the Wyeth family. Her interests extended to more recent developments such as neo-realism and photo-realism, represented by the work of Neil Welliver and Alan Magee.

While Maine is the major theme of the collection, Mrs. Noyce did not restrict her collecting exclusively to images of the state or to the work of artists who painted here. The November Collection includes such subjects as a view of the New Hampshire White Mountains by Albert Bierstadt (p.27), a portrait of a child and her nurse by Mary Cassatt (p.50), and a vibrant depiction of Squam Light on Cape Ann, Massachusetts, an important, early painting by Edward Hopper (p.30). However, her choices never strayed far from New England or the art movements that flowered here.

The foundation of the November Collection was laid with Mrs. Noyce's first acquisitions in the 1970s, but the majority of it was formed in the decade spanning from 1986 to her death. Her achievement is all the more impressive for having been accomplished over such a short period, especially, as it was not based on any extensive prior study of art history or involvement with the art market. Instead, she drew upon personal experience of the creative process and a lifetime interest in history as she entered this new arena.

A native of Auburn, Massachusetts, Elizabeth Bottomley was the youngest of four children raised by a mother who was a school teacher and a father who held down two jobs to bring his family through the Great Depression. From childhood, she exhibited a fierce intelligence and sharp wit, as well as skill at, and love for, needlework and sailing, which would become lifelong avocations. She left Auburn to study literature at Tufts University, with the ambition of becoming a novelist. As a graduation present, she received from her mother

ALVAN FISHER
Camden Harbor

1846

oil on canvas

29 1/4 x 36 3/8 in.

Farnsworth Art Museum

ALBERT BIERSTADT

Autumn Birches
(Approaching Storm)

circa 1860

oil on board

14 x 19 1/2 in.

Portland Museum of Art

her first painting, *Smokey Sou'wester* (1950), a watercolor by George Gale of a boat sailing in the waters off Rhode Island, where she had sailed as a child. It would remain a treasured possession throughout her life, and she relished the story of the artist's dual life—as a painter and illustrator trained at the Rhode Island School of Design and as a seaman on the American and Hawaiian Steamship Line and, later, the Bristol Ferry.

While at Tufts, she joined a summer theatrical production as costume director and met her future husband, Robert Noyce, a member of the cast. At the time, the man who would become an inventor of the integrated circuit and one of the founders of Fairchild Semiconductor and the Intel Corporation was studying for his doctorate in physical electronics at the Massachusetts Institute of Technology. The couple were married in 1952, and for the next two decades Betty Noyce devoted herself to raising four children and following her husband's burgeoning career. That career eventually took the Noyces to a fast-paced life in California with which she was never fully comfortable. As an antidote, she brought her children east in the summers to the sanctuary of a home on the coast of Maine. Her daughter Pendred recalls, "She liked that Maine was not developed at a time when California was developing so rapidly. That was a difference between my mother and father. He liked everything that was new and high-tech. She liked antiques."[2]

The Noyces were divorced in 1975, and Betty chose to settle in Maine because she "missed the New England ethic and the New England rootedness, stability."[3] Heartache and loneliness made it a difficult transition but, ultimately, as her daughter says, "Maine healed her. She loved the rocks and shore. She told me she woke up every morning happy to be here. Maine took her on her own terms without glitz or pretentiousness."[4] Before long, she began repaying the favor by assisting with community projects. She already had a history of public giving, both in California and in Maine, where she had funded construction of a library for the town of Bremen. She soon became involved in efforts as humble as contributing a square to her town's bicentennial quilt and as grand as helping to expand a mid-coast hospital.

When a cause caught her attention, she supported it generously. As she said, "to a cause I care about, I'm going to give as much as I can," adding, "I just hope to make a difference in my own community. Selfishly, I give where my donation will make my immediate environment safer, cleaner, brighter. . . and leave it to others to do as much as they can do in their communities, and that's the way the wider world improves."[5] Betty Noyce defined her neighborhood as Maine, and she nurtured it through charitable gifts to many of the state's major non-profit institutions. She also began practicing what she called "catalytic philanthropy" by investing in Maine businesses and communities with the goal of creating jobs and boosting the economy. When Maine National Bank was lost to the state because its parent company Bank of New England failed, she financed the establishment of Maine Bank and Trust; when she learned of the potential sale of the J.J. Nissen Baking Company to an out-of-state company, she purchased it to keep jobs in Maine.

Elizabeth Noyce christening the Maritime History Building, Maine Maritime Museum, Bath, Maine, 16 June 1989.

One of the first museums to engage her interest was the Maine Maritime Museum. Founded in 1963 and located on the banks of the Kennebec River in Bath, the museum is devoted to preserving, studying, and interpreting Maine's maritime history with collections including paintings, decorative arts, models, charts, instruments, and shipping records. Its focus dovetailed with Mrs. Noyce's interests, both as a sailor and as a student of maritime history. She was invited to join its board at a time when plans for an expansion were underway. Ultimately, she provided the three-and-a-half-million-dollar challenge grant that made possible construction of a new museum facility, which she christened at its opening in 1989.

Mrs. Noyce's association with the Maine Maritime Museum coincided with her growing interest in collecting marine paintings. A fruitful environment for expanding her knowledge of the genre and her connoisseurship skills, the museum offered a fine collection of paintings and experienced collectors on the staff and board of trustees. (Among the latter was Terrance Geaghan, a maker

EDWARD HOPPER
Squam Light

1912

oil on canvas

22 x 29 in.

Private Collection

MARSDEN HARTLEY
Surf on Reef

1937-1938

oil on board

9 7/8 x 14 1/8 in.

Portland Museum of Art

of ship models and a dealer in marine fine art who, over time, came to play a major part in the formation of the November Collection.) Mrs. Noyce joined the museum's collections committee and quickly took on more than an advisory role in the growth of the institution's holdings. On several occasions she purchased for the collection works which staff had presented to the committee with a compelling argument for their relevance to the museum's mission. In each instance, it was a work that would have been impossible for the institution to acquire without assistance. For example, she underwrote the purchase of James E. Buttersworth's dramatic view of *The Clipper Ship Warner Rounding Cape Horn* (ca. 1851). Her generosity enabled the museum to fill a gap in its collection with this rare image of a Maine-made clipper by one of the best-known, mid-nineteenth-century painters of ships.

Mrs. Noyce's appreciation of the importance of such works to the Maine Maritime Museum was informed by her own efforts to build a collection of marine art. Many of her first art acquisitions were paintings and models of ships. These works were a direct extension of her fascination with maritime culture, an interest which also manifested itself in her love of sailing and boats, her taste for literature (fiction and non-fiction) on naval themes, and her efforts to preserve Maine's maritime traditions, ranging from support for the state's island communities to active involvement with the Maine Maritime Academy. Atypically, her gifts to the Maine Maritime Museum took the form of direct purchases rather than works from her own collection. Those came to the museum only in her bequest of nine paintings, which included a rare nineteenth-century portrait of a jury-rigged schooner and contemporary images of coastal life.

Not long after she became involved with the Maine Maritime Museum, the Portland Museum of Art emerged as a new focus of her energy and interest. In 1983, the PMA opened a 62,500-square-foot wing designed by I. M. Pei and Associates, which made it Maine's largest fine arts museum. It also necessitated a ten-million-dollar capital campaign to support the expanded operations. As Betty Noyce recalled when announcing a one-million-dollar lead gift to that campaign, this new association began when Owen Wells (who would become her attorney, advisor, and close friend) "called me cold and asked me to come to Portland and look at the empty building before the galleries were filled because he said it was so architecturally pleasing. I said I didn't think it sounded very interesting. But I came and, of course, it was exciting, engrossing and invigorating." She went on to observe, "I am sophisticated enough to know there would be expenses involved. . . . I made up my mind I would like to be involved."[6]

The Portland Museum of Art focuses on American and European art, primarily of the nineteenth and twentieth centuries, with special emphasis on the development of the visual arts in Maine. It is the latter which distinguishes its collection and which captured Betty Noyce's attention. The state's art history is rich in works by such artists as Fitz Hugh Lane, Frederic Church, Winslow Homer, George Bellows, and John Marin, which simultaneously tell the stories of the emergence of an American artistic tradition and of Maine's changing landscape and the lives of the people who have inhabited it. Mrs. Noyce became captivated by this history and, in time, she forged strong relationships with two other public museums that focus on art in Maine–the Farnsworth Art Museum in Rockland and the Monhegan Museum on the island of the same name. Her associations with those institutions were similarly marked by leadership gifts to expansion campaigns and were founded on her evolving activities as a collector.

By the mid-1980s, Mrs. Noyce's interests had shifted from marine painting to a broader view of Maine's role in American art. The expansion of her collecting focus was heralded in 1986 by the first of her truly substantial acquisitions—Andrew Wyeth's *Bridge at Martinsville* (1939) and Fitz Hugh Lane's *Castine Harbor* (1852) (p.22), which were purchased two days apart. These works mark the beginning of a new level of ambition in her collecting and contain many of the elements that came to characterize the November

FRANK HENRY SHAPLEIGH

Lovel's Pond from Jockey Cap, Fryeburg, Maine

circa 1872

oil on canvas

14 1/4 x 24 1/8 in.

Portland Museum of Art

FREDERIC EDWIN CHURCH
Mount Katahdin from Millinocket Camp

1895

oil on canvas

26 1/2 x 42 1/4 in.

Private Collection

Collection. Painted nearly a century apart, the paintings each present a view of coastal Maine that is serene, silent, beautiful, and luminous. Her attraction to these qualities was echoed repeatedly in future choices.

The Lane was a signal work in other ways. It was the first of four paintings by the Massachusetts-born artist that Mrs. Noyce purchased over an eight-year period, making Lane (along with George Bellows, Charles Woodbury, and Jamie Wyeth) one of the artists that she collected in the greatest depth. Its subject, Castine, was the first town in Maine that Lane visited and a locale that he returned to and painted extensively; it was also a place that Betty Noyce knew well, as a sailor and as a dedicated trustee of the Maine Maritime Academy, which is located there.

Castine Harbor offers a window onto that place in another age. Painted from an island in the harbor, looking toward Dyce Head Light, this tranquil and lovely painting records a bustling port. Lane communicated the nature of the activity centered there through his careful depiction of the vessels in the harbor, chronicling the development of shipping in the nineteenth century. In the right foreground are two small, shallow-draft sailboats of the kind used for fishing and moving cargo locally. To the left are three much larger ships, moored at a deep-water anchorage, which represent the spectrum of mid-nineteenth-century commercial vessels: the swift and sturdy two-masted brigantine on the right, the speedy and graceful schooner on the left (which would, in time, replace the brig in delivering supplies along the coast), and, in the middle, a three-masted merchant ship, a large, deep-water sailing vessel that suggests the glamor of foreign ports and exotic goods.

As a knowledgeable student of maritime history, Betty Noyce read and appreciated the significance of Lane's imagery. The layering of meaning in *Castine Harbor* is another hallmark of works that entered the November Collection. Mrs. Noyce was especially attracted to images that celebrated Maine's elemental beauty while encoding deeper narratives. In her first major purchases, the narratives were usually tied to Maine's maritime heritage. In 1988, a year and a half after she acquired the Lane, she added to her collection

Rockwell Kent's *Wreck of the D. T. Sheridan* (ca. 1949-1953) (p.38) (a painting that became known among her grandchildren as "Granny's canoe"). The work dates to Kent's return to Monhegan Island after a thirty-year absence and is a prime example of his mature style in its intense palette, crisp forms, and emphatic two-dimensionality. The painting depicts the rusting hull of a steel tugboat that had run aground on Monhegan's Lobster Point in a dense fog in November 1948.[7] None of the drama of that event is apparent in Kent's image, yet, in its skeletal stillness, it powerfully conveys man's subordination to the forces of nature.

The narrative import of later acquisitions became subtler, more implicit, and often communicated through associative or metaphorical imagery. Frank Shapleigh's *Lovel's Pond From Jockey Cap, Fryeburg, Maine* (ca. 1872) (p.34) offers a good example. At the most basic level, it is an image of hikers picnicking at the summit of Jockey Cap, overlooking the unspoiled beauty of Maine's interior. The painting extends the Hudson River tradition of transcribing the sublimity of nature and documents the movement of middle class rusticators into the landscape in search of a transcendental experience. But the work also has a deeper historical meaning. Frank Shapleigh's hikers have climbed Jockey Cap to look out on the famous site where, in 1725, Captain John Lovewell was tracked down and killed in retaliation for his brutal raids on Native American settlements. The standing man points to the place where this event occurred on the shore of Saco Pond, which was later renamed for Lovewell. This history was immortalized in the nineteenth century in two poems by Henry Wadsworth Longfellow and a sermon published in the 1860s. It was viewed alternately as a tale of the tragic death of a colonial hero or of justified revenge for his savagery. Seen either way, the painting implicitly tells the story of the bloody cost of the European conquest of North America.

Albert Bierstadt's *Autumn Birches (Approaching Storm)* (ca. 1860) (p.27), one of Mrs. Noyce's last purchases, is an even more distilled case of an artist expressing meaning through a pure image of nature. The painting dates to Bierstadt's visits to the White Mountains in the late 1850s, when he

ROCKWELL KENT

Wreck of the D. T. Sheridan

circa 1949-1953

oil on canvas

27 3/8 x 43 7/8 in.

Portland Museum of Art

GEORGE BELLOWS
Matinicus

1916

oil on canvas

32 x 40 in.

Portland Museum of Art

executed a series of landscapes on portable 14 x 19 $^{1}/_{2}$ inch paperboards. It shows Bierstadt exploring his love of drama and color through two of his favorite themes, autumn and approaching storms. In this instance, his interest in capturing shifting light and season may have been more than a formal exercise. The sense of dark foreboding he creates allies the painting to the many views of impending storms by his contemporaries, all painted, like this one, on the eve of the Civil War.[8]

The issue of an artist's intent fascinated Betty Noyce. When she acquired the work of living artists, she frequently engaged them in direct dialogue either during a studio visit or by inviting them to see her collection. A glimpse of her exchanges about art with artists is preserved in a letter from the painter Alison Hildreth, who wrote expressing gratitude for the opportunity to see the November Collection and pleasure that Mrs. Noyce had given her *Playing Field* (1993) "a good home." In its abstraction *Playing Field* is nearly unique within the collection, but the artist recognized other links between it and Mrs. Noyce's more representational paintings, writing, "a strong sense of light connects all the works. Maine has a particular kind of light and it seems that painters in general react to it."[9]

If an artist was no longer living, Mrs. Noyce sought out works from which his or her purpose could be gleaned. In 1992, she purchased Frederic Church's *Mount Katahdin from Millinocket Camp* (1895) (p.35) at auction in New York. It is, perhaps, his greatest painting of a subject that he had first depicted nearly a half-century earlier. In fact, the work is Church's last major studio painting, begun in 1891 and completed in 1895, in time to be presented to his wife on her fifty-ninth birthday. His majestic presentation of Mount Katahdin, bathed in golden light and soaring above Lake Millinocket, celebrates the beauty of divine creation. However, the canoer paddling in the foreground hints at another message. In a note dedicating the painting to his wife, Church wrote, "I am happy in the belief that owing to your generous, unselfish and cheerful nature the Autumn of your life will be beautiful in its brightness and color. Your old guide is paddling his cause in the shadow, but he knows that the glories of the Heavens and earth are seen more appreciatively when the observer rests in the shade."[10]

Mrs. Noyce's favorite painting in her collection was *Dark Harbor Fishermen* (1943) by N. C. Wyeth (cover), which she acquired in 1990. She was fond of quoting Andrew Wyeth's opinion that it was his father's greatest painting, which confirmed her own sense of the picture. A highly successful illustrator, N.C. Wyeth strove in his paintings to employ his gift for pictorial narrative to create works that resonated with deeper meanings. This ennobling image succeeds by portraying the fishermen as mythic figures and by symbolizing, through their labors, the theme of sustenance (in a seeming allusion to the biblical tale of the loaves and fishes). *Dark Harbor Fishermen* was quickly recognized as a masterpiece and in 1944 was selected by a jury including Rockwell Kent and Fernand Léger for an exhibition, *Portrait of America*, organized by Artists for Victory.[11]

The power that this painting had for Mrs. Noyce as an evocation of a specific time and place was deepened by a letter she received from Fern Dodge, a descendant of the fishermen depicted by Wyeth. Dodge wrote, "The Dark Harbor Fisherman [sic] is of my Grandfather Fernie Dell Barton Which [sic] is sitting in the boat with elbow on knee with the old English cap on. And my other Grandfather Standing [sic] with the oil cloth coveralls yellow on. His name Fred Otis Dodge. And the man knitting the fish is Frankie Dyer. These three men are gone now. The man in back holding the oars I think his name was Carl Pike. And I'm sure he has pasten on also."[12]

Dark Harbor Fishermen was joined by other paintings in the November Collection that celebrated Maine's ethic of simplicity and hard work. One of the greatest is *The Teamster* (p.18), painted by George Bellows during a visit to Maine in the summer of 1916. He portrayed his subject, clad in overalls with his team of draught horses, standing in front of the skeleton of a wooden ship that was being constructed in the Camden shipyards as part of the war effort. It was one of a series of paintings which, Bellows wrote, were "in continual danger of becoming either illustration or melodrama" but had "nevertheless in

FRANK W. BENSON
Portrait of Parker R. Stone

1922

oil on canvas

30 1/4 x 25 1/4 in.

Farnsworth Art Museum

SUSAN PAINE

Portrait of Mr. J. H. Corbett

1831

oil on panel

29 7/8 x 24 3/8 in.

Portland Museum of Art

SUSAN PAINE

Portrait of Mrs. J. H. Corbett

1831

oil on panel

29 15/16 x 24 5/16 in.

Portland Museum of Art

several cases evolved into very rare pictures."[13] Indeed, *The Teamster* is an epic American painting, imbued with the values of honesty, strength, industriousness, and loyalty.

This interest in human experience led Mrs. Noyce to begin collecting portraits in the 1990s. She acquired two striking works by Frank Benson, *Portrait of Ellie* (1927) and *Portrait of Parker R. Stone* (1922) (p.42), both of which were painted on North Haven Island, where the artist and his family summered for forty years. Intrigued by Benson and his work, Mrs. Noyce traveled to North Haven to visit the artist's studio and to meet his descendants. She was charmed to learn that *Portrait of Ellie* is a depiction of Benson's grandchild and bears a dedication to her father, "Max Rogers." Family history has it that it was painted when the three-year-old wandered into the barn to watch her grandfather at work. Without warning, Benson stopped, picked her up, and put her on a stool in view of his easel–the painting captures the startled expression of a child told suddenly and gruffly to sit still. It would be the last portrait Benson would paint of a grandchild because, he said, "I'm too old and you wiggle too much."[14]

Parker Stone, a year-round resident of North Haven, was one of Benson's "oldest and most valued friends."[15] Their friendship was founded on a mutual love of boating, hunting, and fishing. In his portrait, Stone wears an expression of wariness that suggests uncertainty about the new surroundings of the artist's studio.

Many of the images of people in the November Collection–whether formal portraits or genre scenes–held personal associations for Mrs. Noyce. When showing Charles Woodbury's *Ogunquit Bath House with Lady and Dog* (ca. 1912) (p.46) to guests, she would laughingly observe that it was a portrait of her. Woodbury's depiction of a woman, dressed in heavy clothing and absorbed in sewing, with her back turned to a beach crowded with sunbathers, recalls Mrs. Noyce's joking observation that she would be more inclined to give money to a cause "if that guaranteed that I could stay home, all alone."[16]

In choosing an oil by Winslow Homer, she did not seek out a view of Maine's coast, but opted instead for *Enchanted* (1874) (p.47), from his series of images of children painted before his move to Maine. She herself was enchanted by the artist's depiction of the little girl's mesmerizing power over her two male companions.

Works by women and of women formed an area of special interest for Betty Noyce. More than thirty women artists are represented in the November Collection, including Mary Cassatt, Beverly Hallam, Anna Eliza Hardy, Emily Muir, Louise Nevelson, Susan Paine, Gertrude Fiske, and Marguerite Zorach. The Cassatt, *Anne and Her Nurse* (ca. 1897) (p.50), was a favorite of the collector and hung in a place of honor in her bedroom. This tender portrait of a tired child resting in the arms of her nurse spoke to Mrs. Noyce's own memories of raising her children. At the same time, it is an emblem of Mary Cassatt's determination to succeed, on her own terms, in an art world dominated by men. Cassatt earned the distinction of being one of only two women, and the only American, to exhibit with the French Impressionists in the 1870s. Like her Impressionist colleagues, she focused on the world of everyday life which, in her case, was the domestic realm of women and children.

The unusual story of Susan Paine, represented in the November Collection by portraits of Mr. and Mrs. J. H. Corbett (1831) (p.43), was equally intriguing to Mrs. Noyce. Paine was part of an expanding population of itinerant artists traveling through New England's countryside in the early nineteenth century, who both stimulated and supplied a growing demand for painted likenesses among a newly prosperous rural middle class. A career as an itinerant painter offered occupational and social mobility, which was especially attractive to young men of entrepreneurial spirit and social ambition; it was rare for a woman to pursue a life of itinerancy. As recounted in her 1854 autobiography, *Roses and Thorns*, Susan Paine was driven to support herself as a traveling painter (drawing on little more than school-girl training in the ornamental arts) after divorcing her "taunting, sneering, surly tyrant" of a husband

CHARLES WOODBURY

Ogunquit Bath House with Lady and Dog

circa 1912

oil on canvas board

11 7/8 x 17 in.

Portland Museum of Art

WINSLOW HOMER
Enchanted

1874

oil on canvas

12 1/4 x 20 1/4 in.

Private Collection

(another uncommon event in early nineteenth-century New England). In 1826, she moved to Portland from Providence, Rhode Island, and began soliciting commissions through the local press, advertising that she charged eight dollars for a portrait in oils and four dollars for a crayon likeness.[17] She wintered in Portland but traveled to rural Maine communities in the other seasons. In 1831, she visited Lisbon Falls, where she painted portraits of the Corbetts and other townspeople. The title of her book came from this experience; as she wrote, "Like many other inland places, the inhabitants were fond of display; without possessing too much liberality, or genuine refinement; but there were some exceptions. (Roses grown among thorns.) I found a few in this place, that I shall ever remember with the sincerest feelings of friendship and esteem."[18]

It is unknown what Susan Paine felt about Horace and Catherine Cheney Corbett, but her likenesses preserve a careful record of the couple. He is dressed in a stylish yet conservative fashion suitable for the prosperous owner of a woolen mill. His bearing exudes confidence, and the newspaper in his grasp hints at his interactions with the wider world. (It may indicate more—the partially visible title, "New England Gal...," suggests that he holds a copy of *The New England Galaxy and Masonic Magazine*, which may symbolize membership in the Freemasons.) Similarly, Mrs. Corbett wears fashionable but modest clothing appropriate to a woman in her early thirties, the wife of an affluent businessman, and the mother of four children. She is seated by a window in a residential interior with her sewing tools carefully arrayed before her, signifying her largely domestic and maternal role. The table placed in front of her masks the fact that she is seven months pregnant–her portrait was completed on January 3, 1831, and on March 6 that year she gave birth to her fifth child.[19] Sadly, her portrait too quickly took on a memorial role, for Catherine Corbett "departed this life on Tuesday the 4th Decr 1832 at about one o'clock in the morning aged 33 years."[20]

When showing this pair of portraits, Betty Noyce preferred to discuss Mrs. Corbett's likeness. She recognized that a pin cushion, a pair of scissors, two spools of thread, and a thimble could speak volumes about a life. The portraits were hung above a display of her collection of period sewing tools, an offshoot of her own skill with the needle. A favorite pastime of Mrs. Noyce's was creating appliqué pictures from scraps of fabric. These scenes—of quilting bees, garden parties, art exhibitions, and children at play—revealed her as a keen observer of human nature with a sharp sense of humor and an eye for gesture, color, and texture. Her fabric pictures were a creative outlet that deepened her appreciation of the role sewing had historically played in women's lives, providing a vehicle for personal expression within the confines of domestic responsibilities. This interest in needlework is evident in other paintings in the November Collection, such as *Loving Stitches* (ca. 1908) (p.51), William Wallace Gilchrist's intimate portrait of his wife sewing by lamplight.

The acquisition of the Paine portraits sheds light on the process by which Betty Noyce built and refined her collection. Six months before their purchase, a pair of portraits by another Maine-based non-academic artist, William Matthew Prior, entered the November Collection. Her interest in Prior and the history of itinerant artists in Maine had been piqued when she saw an example of his work in a 1993 exhibition at the Portland Museum of Art. Through the Museum's staff, she learned that a rare pair of portraits, signed and dated by the artist, would be coming up at auction in October of that year. In addition to being unusually well-documented examples of Prior's work, the portraits of Joseph Sewall, Jr., and Eliza Sewall (1838) came with extensive histories of their subjects who had been eminent residents of Bath. (When he sat for his portrait, Joseph Sewall was in the fourth of his eight years as the collector of customs for the Port of Bath, an appointment of President Andrew Jackson.) Betty Noyce signalled her intent to pursue them in a laconic note, "Thanks for. . . the Matthew Prior info. Like the look of those portraits."[21] She was the successful bidder, and the paintings took a place of prominence in her front hall until they were replaced the following April by the Paine portraits. With the acquisition of a pair of non-academic likenesses even more in concert

WILLIAM MATTHEW PRIOR
Portrait of Eliza Sewall (top)
Portrait of Joseph Sewall (bottom)

1838

oil on canvas

Portland Museum of Art

MARY CASSATT
Anne and Her Nurse

circa 1897

oil on canvas

27 1/2 x 23 1/2 in.

Portland Museum of Art

WILLIAM WALLACE GILCHRIST, JR.
Loving Stitches

circa 1908

gouache, watercolor, and pastel on board

29 x 21 3/16 in.

Portland Museum of Art

with her personal interests, the Priors became redundant. In June, she thoughtfully donated them to the Portland Museum of Art in recognition of the role its staff had played in their purchase.

The clearcut linearity of this sequence of events was rarely repeated, but it does typify several characteristics of Betty Noyce's collecting. As do most collectors, she expanded her knowledge with each purchase. When a work by a new artist or a painting in a new style entered the November Collection, it was often the catalyst for future acquisitions of pieces by the artist or the artist's peers, or works showing the development of the style or movement. The progression of her acquisitions is characterized by this initial attraction to a work followed by careful study of its historical context. She learned about art by staying current with the literature, maintaining associations with dealers and museums, and, frequently, making pilgrimages to sites associated with artists, such as Monhegan Island, Ogunquit, and the Isles of Shoals.

Mrs. Noyce's acquisition of a significant group of Maine paintings by Robert Henri and several of his students and friends offers a case in point. After her 1988 purchase of Rockwell Kent's *Wreck of the D. T. Sheridan* (p.38), she rounded out her Kent holdings in 1993 by securing a rare, early Monhegan painting, *Maine Coast* (ca. 1907) (p.2). A masterpiece, this was part of a group of paintings Kent created during two years of intensive activity on Monhegan–works that launched his career when they were exhibited in New York in 1907. These two paintings introduced Betty Noyce to the history of Kent and his peers in Maine and led to the acquisition of still more works.[22] Kent had first visited Monhegan at the encouragement of his teacher, Robert Henri. Not long after, other members of Henri's circle made their way to Maine, including George Bellows, Randall Davey, Edward Hopper, and Leon Kroll. In 1993, paintings by Bellows (p.39), Henri (p.54), and Kroll also came into the November Collection. Coincident with, but independent of this, the Portland Museum of Art began planning an exhibition on this subject, *The Allure of the Maine Coast: Robert Henri and His Circle, 1903-1918.*[23] Mrs. Noyce agreed early on to support this project with loans from her collection, and during the next two years she acquired other related paintings by Bellows (p.18), Davey, Henri, Hopper (p.19), and Kroll. In the midst of this activity, she sailed to Monhegan Island "to stroll around the territory which has inspired so many"; the trip included visits to Kent's studio, the other houses he designed and built on the island, and the sites where he and his friends painted.[24]

Rachel Armstrong, Elizabeth Noyce, and Bill Boynton, Monhegan Island, Maine, 13 June 1995

The pattern evident in this chronology represents only one piece of Mrs. Noyce's collecting activity in this period; she was simultaneously developing other aspects of her collection. One of these was a broader representation of work created by artists on Monhegan Island. This was certainly related to her interest in Kent, Henri, and their associates, but it was also strongly influenced by her growing involvement with the Monhegan Museum. In the mid-1990s, she became actively engaged in that museum's efforts to preserve the social and artistic history of the island, which led her to make a challenge grant of half the funds needed to construct a gallery for its art collection. At the same time, she began to place new emphasis on seeking out and acquiring works by the full scope of Monhegan's artists. Of the twenty paintings that she bequeathed to the museum, by Jay Connaway, James Fitzgerald, Eric Hudson, Edward Redfield (p.55), Samuel Triscott, and others, seventeen were acquired between 1993 and 1996.

As a collector, Betty Noyce had an unusual ability to select works that served two apparently contradictory goals. She consistently chose pieces that manifested her tastes and interests but, at the same time, she seems always to have collected with an eye toward eventual gifts. Even as she lived with and derived great personal pleasure from all of the works in her collection, they were being catalogued, conserved, and organized for dispersal to specific beneficiaries. Quietly, she analyzed the needs of the institutions that she cared about fostering, and factored those needs into her collecting decisions. Occasionally,

ROBERT HENRI
Rocks and Sea

1911

oil on panel

11 1/2 x 15 in.

Portland Museum of Art

EDWARD WILLIS REDFIELD

The Toymaker's Home (Monhegan Island, Maine)

1928

oil on canvas

26 1/8 x 32 1/4 in.

Monhegan Museum

she was guided by a specific cue, as when she purchased Charles Demuth's *Cluster* (1922) from the I.B.M. Collection after the Farnsworth's collections committee admired it in the Sotheby's auction catalogue.

She rarely gave these institutions any hint of her plans. For example, while working with the Maine Maritime Academy on the development of a humanities curriculum, she independently began to seek out art that would ultimately have a place there. With this in mind, she purchased Thomas Fransioli's view of *Dennett's Wharf, Castine* (1946) (p.58). Fransioli's serene depiction of academy cadets in formation on Castine's waterfront has a poetic resonance–it is a record of an institution established in 1941 to train naval officers for service in World War II, from the hand of a veteran of that war. On his return from Japan, Fransioli had sought out the solace of his family's summer home in Castine; as he remembers, "The peace and calm, after seeing and being in destroyed Manila and bombed and burned up Tokyo, was unbelievable."[25]

During her lifetime, Mrs. Noyce periodically made gifts from her collection to Maine's museums. Her decisions about gifts were guided both by an understanding of each institution's needs and by her evolving sense of the November Collection. The collection was being continually refined–some of the works that matured out of it were donated to museums, while others were sold. (For example, when she secured a Maine watercolor by Edward Hopper (p.19) for the collection, an earlier purchase of a Vermont painting by the artist went back into the marketplace.) Consistent with her approach to collecting, gifts were generally made very quietly. Her first contribution to the Portland Museum of Art's collection, Andrew Wyeth's *Raven's Grove* (1985) (p.59), was made anonymously in 1991. Subsequent gifts came in her name, but she generally preferred that little fanfare accompany them.

It was only in the last year of her life that Mrs. Noyce's giving became visible and public. In June 1996, she offered to help the Portland Museum of Art recognize the dedicated service to the Museum of her friends Roger and Katherine Woodman by donating Cassatt's *Anne and Her Nurse* (p.50) in their honor. She chose to make the presentation personally, artfully orchestrating a surprise that caused a sensation at the annual trustees' dinner. Similarly, the following month she gave a childhood portrait of Maine Governor Percival Baxter and his sister Madeleine to the Maine State Museum. She presented the painting, *Babes in the Woods* (ca. 1882) by Eastman Johnson and Jervis McEntee, to Governor Angus King at a press conference. In giving it, she said that she liked to imagine that Baxter, who created the 200,000-acre Baxter State Park, was saying to his sister "What might you do with all these woods?"[26]

Both of these gifts show how carefully Betty Noyce made matches between works from her collection and the missions of the museums and causes she supported. Her refined understanding of each museum's purpose and the strengths and weaknesses of its collection is even more evident in the thoughtful planning that went into her bequest. In part, she distributed the paintings geographically, returning works to the regions where they were created or that they depict. The majority of the collection was given to the Farnsworth Art Museum and the Portland Museum of Art, and when there was more than one work by an American master they were usually divided between the two. Augmenting both of these strategies was Mrs. Noyce's perception of how the November Collection could both complete and be completed by aspects of these institutions' holdings. In the process, she transformed their collections in a way that is far beyond what they could have achieved on their own. It was one more fulfillment of her belief that the world improves when people share and work together.

In many ways, Betty Noyce was not a typical art collector. She was not motivated by acquisitiveness or a sense of competition. She did not collect with an aesthetic or political agenda in mind, nor were her activities as a collector an outgrowth of a lifetime involvement with the arts. She had no ambition to construct a memorial to herself. However, like many collectors, she did create something akin to a physical manifestation of her world view. She chose New England because it embodied the values of strength, individuality, fellowship, and endurance that she admired and lived by; she chose art that reinforced

THOMAS FRANSIOLI

Dennett's Wharf, Castine

1946

oil on canvas

24 1/8 x 29 15/16 in.

Maine Maritime Academy

ANDREW WYETH
Raven's Grove

1985

tempera on masonite

31 x 27 5/8 in.

Portland Museum of Art

those deeply held beliefs. She had come to rest in Maine and found comfort in paintings that captured the serenity, peace, and harmony that she experienced here. The November Collection is a potent expression of Betty Noyce's desire to surround herself with beauty and to extend herself to the people of Maine. It is, in the end, a paean to the art of Maine: the landscape that inspires it, the artists who create it, and the people and institutions that preserve it.

1 Much of the November Collection was seen publicly in two exhibitions at the Farnsworth Art Museum and the Portland Museum of Art: *An Eye for Maine: Paintings from a Private Collection* (1994) and *A Brush with Greatness: American Watercolors from the November Collection* (1996).

2 "Modestly she handed out millions," *Boston Globe*, 26 September 1996, p. B2.

3 "Philanthropist Noyce dies, stunning state," *Portland Press Herald*, 19 September 1996, p. 6A.

4 "State bids goodbye to 'best friend'," *Portland Press Herald*, 24 September 1996, p. 8A.

5 "State bids goodbye," p. 8A.

6 "Art museum receives $1 million gift," *Portland Press Herald*, 20 June 1984, p. 14.

7 William P. Quinn, *Shipwrecks Around Maine* (Orleans, MA: The Lower Cape Publishing Co., 1983), pp. 122-123.

8 See David C. Miller, "The Iconology of Wrecked or Stranded Boats in Mid- to Late Nineteenth-Century Art," in *American Iconology* (New Haven: Yale University Press, 1993).

9 Alison Hildreth to Elizabeth Noyce, November 1994, Portland Museum of Art object file.

10 Frederic Church, undated note, Olana, Hudson, New York.

11 Information courtesy of the N. C. Wyeth Project, Brandywine River Museum, Chadds Ford, Pennsylvania.

12 Fern Dodge to Maine Maritime Museum Shop, 27 February 1995, photocopy in PMA object file.

13 George Bellows to Robert Henri, 8 September 1916, Henri Papers, The Yale Collection of American Literature, Beinecke Rare Book and Manuscript Library, Yale University.

14 Interview with Jane Guthrie, North Haven Island, Maine, 27 August 1996.

15 Frank Benson to Parker Stone, 25 March 1947, photocopy in Farnsworth Art Museum object file.

16 "State bids goodbye," p. 8A.

17 Gael May McKibben and William David Barry, *Women Pioneers in Maine Art* (Portland, ME: The Joan Whitney Payson Gallery of Art, 1981), p. 13.

18 Susan Paine, *Roses and Thorns: or, Recollections of an Artist* (1854), p. 158.

19 The painting of Mrs. Corbett is inscribed on the reverse in the artist's hand: "Mrs. C. Corbitt/ By Susan Paine/ Jan 3 1831"; *Lisbon, Maine, Vital Records* (Camden, ME: Picton Press, 1995), p. 51.

20 *Lisbon, Maine, Vital Records*, p. 51.

21 Elizabeth Noyce to Jessica Nicoll, 16 October 1993, PMA object file.

22 It is likely that this new collecting direction was influenced by a publication that elegantly explores the influence of Winslow Homer on this generation of artists: Bruce Robertson, *Reckoning with Winslow Homer* (Cleveland, OH: Cleveland Museum of Art, 1990).

23 Works from The November Collection included in the exhibition are listed in the catalogue: Jessica Nicoll, *The Allure of the Maine Coast: Robert Henri and His Circle in Maine, 1903-1918* (Portland, ME: Portland Museum of Art, 1995).

24 Elizabeth Noyce to Jessica Nicoll, 18 May 1995, PMA donor file.

25 Thomas Fransioli to Stuart Feld, Hirschl & Adler Galleries, 30 November 1986, Hirschl & Adler archives, New York, New York.

26 Elizabeth Noyce quoted in "Painting of Percival Baxter given to state," *Brunswick Times Record*, 30 July 1996, p. 5.

CHECKLIST

The November Collection

Works from the November Collection now in public collections. Dimensions are given in inches, with height preceding width. Unless otherwise noted, works were donated in the 1996 bequest of Elizabeth B. Noyce.

JOEL BABB
United States, born 1947

Leviathans: The Bath Iron Works, 1994
oil on canvas
36 x 65
Maine Maritime Academy (1995 gift)

GEORGE BELLOWS
United States, 1882-1925

The Fish Wharf, Matinicus Island, 1916
oil on panel
18 x 22
Farnsworth Art Museum

Matinicus, 1916 (p.39)
oil on canvas
32 x 40
Portland Museum of Art

The Teamster, 1916 (p.18)
oil on canvas
34 x 44
Farnsworth Art Museum

FRANK W. BENSON
United States, 1862-1951

Portrait of Parker R. Stone, 1922 (p.42)
oil on canvas
30 1/4 x 25 1/4
Farnsworth Art Museum

Rescue, n.d.
gouache and charcoal on card
8 5/8 x 12 1/2
Farnsworth Art Museum

ALBERT BIERSTADT
United States (born Germany), 1830-1902

Autumn Birches (Approaching Storm), circa 1860 (p.27)
oil on board
14 x 19 1/2
Portland Museum of Art

DWIGHT BLANEY
United States, 1865-1944

The Jeanette, 1901
oil on canvas
22 1/8 x 26 1/8
Farnsworth Art Museum (1996 gift)

ALFRED THOMPSON BRICHER
United States, 1837-1908

Coastal Scene (Bay of Fundy, Canada) Ships Along the Shore, circa 1885-1890
oil on canvas
15 13/16 x 32
Portland Museum of Art

Mt. Kearsarge from Intervale, 1864
oil on paper on aluminum
5 9/16 x 9 7/16
Portland Museum of Art

HARRISON BIRD BROWN
United States, 1831-1915

Natural Pool, circa 1860-1880
oil on canvas
12 3/4 x 24 3/4
Portland Museum of Art

Seascape, circa 1860-1880
oil on ivory
2 1/2 x 4
Portland Museum of Art

MARY CASSATT
United States, 1844-1926

Anne and Her Nurse, circa 1897 (p.50)
oil on canvas
27 1/2 x 23 1/2
Portland Museum of Art (1996 gift in honor of Roger and Katherine Woodman)

CLARENCE CHATTERTON
United States, 1880-1973

Road to Ogunquit, circa 1940
oil on masonite
17 1/4 x 24 1/8
Portland Museum of Art
Gift of Pendred E. Noyce (1997)

JAY CONNAWAY
United States, 1893-1970

Baiting–Interior, mid-twentieth century
oil on paper mounted on panel
16 x 20
Monhegan Museum

Crashing Spray, mid-twentieth century
oil on masonite
14 x 20
Monhegan Museum

Moonlight Village, Monhegan,
mid-twentieth century
oil on masonite
24 x 36
Monhegan Museum

ELEANOR PARKE CUSTIS
United States, 1897-1983

Damariscove Houses, 1924
gouache on paper
13 3/8 x 15 1/2 (sight)
Farnsworth Art Museum

CARL G. CUTLER
United States, 1873-1945

Pond Island and Camden Hills, circa 1920
watercolor on paper
16 7/8 x 24
Farnsworth Art Museum

RANDALL DAVEY
United States, 1887-1964

View from White Head, Monhegan, 1911
oil on board
11 3/4 x 15
Farnsworth Art Museum

CHARLES DEMUTH
United States, 1883-1935

Cluster, 1922
watercolor and graphite on paper
13 3/4 x 11 3/4
Farnsworth Art Museum

JAN MARINUS DOMELA
United States, 1896-1973

Monhegan Island, 1938
oil on canvas
30 x 40
Farnsworth Art Museum

CHARLES EBERT
United States, 1873-1959

The Old Fishing Boat, n.d.
oil on panel
12 x 15 7/8
Farnsworth Art Museum

[MRS.?] A. CLIVE EDWARDS
United States, active 1920s

Taria Topan, 1925
oil on canvas
22 x 32
Maine Maritime Museum

STEPHEN ETNIER
United States, 1903-1984

Bill I Bibber's Fish House, 1967
oil on canvas
13 x 21
Maine Maritime Museum

The Windlass, 1967-68
oil on canvas
16 x 36 1/4
Maine Maritime Museum

ALVAN FISHER
United States, 1792-1863

Camden Harbor, 1846 (p.26)
oil on canvas
29 1/4 x 36 3/8
Farnsworth Art Museum (1995 gift)

GERTRUDE FISKE
United States, 1878-1961

Foggy Ogunquit, circa 1910s
oil on board
10 x 14
Portland Museum of Art

Silver Maple, Ogunquit, circa 1920s
oil on canvas
24 x 30
Portland Museum of Art

Wells Congregational Church, Wells, Maine,
circa 1920s
oil on canvas
20 1/16 x 27
Portland Museum of Art

FITZ HUGH LANE

Camden Mountains from the South Entrance to the Harbor

1859

oil on canvas

22 1/8 x 36 1/4 in.

Farnsworth Art Museum

JAMES FITZGERALD
United States, 1899-1971

Gulls of Monhegan, circa 1950s
watercolor on paper
21 5/8 x 17 5/8
Monhegan Museum

Mountain Shadows (Katahdin), circa 1950s
watercolor on paper
22 1/2 x 27 1/2
Portland Museum of Art

Plow Horses, circa 1950s
watercolor on paper
22 1/4 x 30 5/8
Portland Museum of Art

JOHN FOLINSBEE
United States, 1892-1972

Friendship, Maine, circa 1937
oil on canvasboard
10 x 14
Portland Museum of Art

THOMAS FRANSIOLI
United States, born 1906

Dennett's Wharf, Castine, 1946 (p.58)
oil on canvas
24 1/8 x 29 15/16
Maine Maritime Academy

LINDEN FREDERICK
United States, born 1953

Bee Hives, 1992
oil on canvas
26 x 26
Farnsworth Art Museum

Yellow Door, 1992
oil on panel, 5 1/2 x 10 3/16
Farnsworth Art Museum

WILLIAM WALLACE GILCHRIST, JR.
United States, 1879-1926

Loving Stitches, circa 1908 (p.51)
gouache, watercolor, and pastel on board
29 x 21 3/16
Portland Museum of Art (1996 gift)

HENRY GOODWIN
United States, 19th century

Otter Cliff, Mt. Desert Island, 1872
oil on canvas
6 5/8 x 10 7/16
Farnsworth Art Museum

Mount Desert, Maine, 1882
oil on canvas
6 1/2 x 10 3/8
Farnsworth Art Museum

VICTOR DE GRAILLY
France, 1804-1889

Eastport and Passamaquoddy Bay, circa 1842
oil on canvas
17 1/4 x 23 1/2
Portland Museum of Art (1995 gift)

ABBOTT FULLER GRAVES
United States, 1859-1936

Snow Along the Coast, early 20th century
oil on canvas
14 x 10
Portland Museum of Art

BEVERLY HALLAM
United States, born 1923

Fallen Petal, 1990
acrylic on linen
19 x 20 1/8
Portland Museum of Art

MARK HALTOF
United States, born 1948

Terracotta Pot, 1987
oil on canvas
18 1/8 x 28 1/8
Portland Museum of Art

ANNA ELIZA HARDY
United States, 1839-1934

Blackberries, n.d.
oil on canvas
16 x 12
Farnsworth Art Museum (1996 gift)

Pansies, n.d.
oil on canvas
11 3/16 x 27
Farnsworth Art Museum (1996 gift)

DEWITT HARDY
United States, born 1940

Seed Pack, 1988
watercolor on paper
13 3/16 x 10 1/8
Portland Museum of Art

VINCENT HARTGEN
United States, born 1914

Morning Gold, Alton Bog, 1994
watercolor on paper
22 15/16 x 34 15/16
Farnsworth Art Museum

Roots Growing out of Rock Fissures, 1993
graphite on paper
25 5/8 x 35 11/16
Farnsworth Art Museum

MARSDEN HARTLEY
United States, 1877-1943

Song of Winter No. 6, circa 1908-1909 (p.70)
oil on board
8 7/8 x 11 7/8
Farnsworth Art Museum (1996 gift)

Surf on Reef, 1937-1938 (p.31)
oil on board
9 7/8 x 14 1/8
Portland Museum of Art

FREDERICK CHILDE HASSAM
United States, 1859-1935

Isles of Shoals, 1915 (p.6)
oil on canvas
25 x 30
Portland Museum of Art

Seascape, 1906
oil on canvas
18 x 22
Portland Museum of Art

JOHN HELIKER
United States, born 1909

Maine Interior with Stove, circa 1968
oil on paper on panel
17 x 16 1/2
Farnsworth Art Museum

Morning Landscape, Cranberry, circa 1978 and 1992-93
oil on canvas
30 x 40
Farnsworth Art Museum

ROBERT HENRI
United States, 1865-1929

Barnacles on Rocks, 1903
oil on panel
8 x 10
Portland Museum of Art

Picnic, Monhegan Island, 1918
crayon on paper
12 x 20
Monhegan Museum

Rocks and Sea, 1911 (p.54)
oil on panel
11 1/2 x 15
Portland Museum of Art

Untitled (The Gray Woods), 1911
oil on panel
15 x 11 3/4
Portland Museum of Art
Gift of Pendred E. Noyce (1997)

ALDRO THOMPSON HIBBARD
United States, 1886-1972

Autumn, mid-20th century
oil on canvas
28 x 36
Portland Museum of Art

ALISON HILDRETH
United States, born 1934

Playing Field, 1993
oil on canvas
24 1/8 x 24
Portland Museum of Art

EMIL HOLZHAUER
United States (born Germany), 1887-1986

Frank Pierce Dressing Fish, mid-20th century
oil on masonite
23 3/4 x 20
Monhegan Museum

WINSLOW HOMER
United States, 1836-1910

Pulling the Dory, circa 1880
watercolor and graphite on paper on board
8 7/16 x 13 1/4
Farnsworth Art Museum

MAURICE BRAZIL PRENDERGAST
Group of Boats (Watching the Regatta)

1907

watercolor and graphite on paper

11 1/2 x 15 1/4 in.

Portland Museum of Art

ROSS STERLING TURNER
Rose Rambler

1907

oil on canvas

27 x 20 1/8 in.

Portland Museum of Art

EDWARD HOPPER
United States, 1882-1967

Lime Rock Quarry No. 1, 1926 (p.19)
watercolor on paper
14 x 20
Farnsworth Art Museum

Railroad Crossing, Rockland, Maine, 1926
watercolor on paper
13 1/2 x 19 3/16
Farnsworth Art Museum

ERIC HUDSON
United States, 1864-1932

Schooner with Dories, early 20th century
oil on canvas
14 1/8 x 11
Monhegan Museum

FREDERICK S. HYND
United States, 1905-1965

View of Lubec, Maine, circa 1960
watercolor on paper
21 x 30 1/8 (sight)
Farnsworth Art Museum

EASTMAN JOHNSON
United States, 1824-1906

April Woods, Logging Camp Scene, circa 1868
oil on canvas
12 x 20 1/8
Farnsworth Art Museum

EASTMAN JOHNSON
AND JERVIS McENTEE
United States, 1824-1906 and 1828-1891

Babes in the Woods, 1882
oil on canvas
30 3/8 x 24 1/4
The Maine State Museum (1996 gift)

ROCKWELL KENT
United States, 1882-1971

Maine Coast, circa 1907 (p.2)
oil on canvas
28 1/8 x 38
Farnsworth Art Museum

Wreck of the D. T. Sheridan, circa 1949-1953 (p.38)
alt. title: ***Wreck of the McKinley***
oil on canvas
27 3/8 x 43 7/8
Portland Museum of Art

WILLIAM KIENBUSCH
United States, 1914-1980

Quarry Hill, Hurricane Island, 1955
casein on paper
21 3/4 x 27 1/2
Farnsworth Art Museum

CHARLES FREDERICK KIMBALL
United States, 1831-1903

Rocks, Wildflowers and Fence, 1883
oil on canvas
12 x 18
Portland Museum of Art

Tidal Pool and Spar, 1883
oil on canvas
12 1/8 x 18 1/8
Portland Museum of Art

LEON KROLL
United States, 1884-1974

Crashing Waves, Ogunquit, 1915
oil on panel
4 1/8 x 4 15/16
Farnsworth Art Museum

Lowering Day, Camden, 1916
oil on canvas
26 3/16 x 32 1/8
Farnsworth Art Museum

MAX KUEHNE
United States (born Germany), 1880-1968

Rockport Harbor, Maine, 1919
oil on canvas
31 x 36 1/8
Farnsworth Art Museum

WALT KUHN
United States, 1877-1949

Landscape with Cows, 1922
oil on canvas
11 1/8 x 16 1/8
Portland Museum of Art

FITZ HUGH LANE
United States, 1804-1865

Camden Mountains from the South Entrance to the Harbor, 1859 (p.63)
oil on canvas
22 1/8 x 36 1/4
Farnsworth Art Museum

Castine Harbor, 1852 (p.22)
oil on canvas
20 1/8 x 30 1/8
Portland Museum of Art

New England Coastal View, 1848
oil on canvas
20 1/16 x 30 1/8
Portland Museum of Art (1995 gift)

Owl's Head Light, Rockland, Maine, circa 1856
oil on canvas
20 1/8 x 33 1/8
Farnsworth Art Museum

BERNARD LANGLAIS
United States, 1921-1977

Sea Gulls, 1977
mixed media on canvas
24 1/16 x 30 1/8
Farnsworth Art Museum

Summer Music, n.d.
oil on board
16 x 20
Farnsworth Art Museum (1996 gift)

MICHAEL H. LEWIS
United States, born 1941

First Light, 1991
turpentine wash on board
4 1/8 x 4 1/6
Portland Museum of Art

Summer Green, 1992
turpentine wash on board
7 3/4 x 7 3/4
Portland Museum of Art

Winter (Orono, Maine) #3, 1990
turpentine wash on board
12 13/16 x 12 13/16
Portland Museum of Art

CABOT LYFORD
United States, born 1925

Red Hen, 1993
granite
21 x 18 x 12 1/2
Portland Museum of Art

JOHN MARIN
United States, 1870-1953

Boat Fantasy, Deer Isle, Maine, No. 30, 1928 (p.11)
watercolor and crayon on paper
18 x 23 1/8
Portland Museum of Art

Fishboat, No. 1 at Eastport, Maine Coast, 1933
watercolor and graphite on paper
14 1/4 x 13 3/4
Farnsworth Art Museum

Pine Tree, Small Point, Maine, 1926
watercolor on paper
17 1/4 x 22
Portland Museum of Art

HENRIK MAYER
United States, 1908-1972

Trefethen House, mid-20th century
oil on panel
10 x 12
Monhegan Museum

ROBERT ERIC MOORE
United States, born 1927

Rocks, Shells and Surf, n.d.
watercolor on paper
19 7/8 x 39 5/16
Farnsworth Art Museum

MARSDEN HARTLEY
Song of Winter No.6

circa 1908-1909

oil on board

8 7/8 x 11 7/8 in.

Farnsworth Art Museum

CARL SPRINCHORN
Gloria October, Shin Pond, Maine

1946

oil on canvas

26 x 34 in.

Portland Museum of Art

EMILY LANSINGH MUIR
United States, born 1904

Quarriers, 1939
watercolor on paper
13 1/2 x 19 1/2 (sight)
Farnsworth Art Museum

Stonington, n.d.
stone mosaic
29 x 148 1/2
Farnsworth Art Museum

Stonington, circa 1940
watercolor on paper
13 3/4 x 20 1/4
Farnsworth Art Museum

Town Dock, Stonington, n.d.
oil on canvas
19 1/2 x 25 5/8 (sight)
Farnsworth Art Museum

Women's Work, 1933
watercolor on paper
13 7/16 x 19 7/16 (sight)
Farnsworth Art Museum

WILLIAM MUIR
United States, 1902-1964

Fish Packing Plant, 1945
watercolor on paper
14 5/8 x 19 5/8 (sight)
Farnsworth Art Museum

HERMANN DUDLEY MURPHY
United States, 1867-1945

Tulips, 1889
oil on canvas
24 1/8 x 20 1/8
Portland Museum of Art

Zinnias and Marigolds, 1932 (p.74)
oil on panel
16 x 12
Portland Museum of Art

LOUISE NEVELSON
United States (born Russia), 1900-1988

Still Life, 1933
oil on board
23 7/8 x 17 13/16
Portland Museum of Art (1995 gift)

JOSEPH NICOLETTI
United States (born Italy), born 1948

Brunswick Mall, 1976
oil on board
5 5/8 x 7 5/8
Portland Museum of Art

Night Still Life, 1990 (p.75)
oil on canvas
50 x 40
Portland Museum of Art

SUSAN (OR SUSANNAH) PAINE
United States, 1792-1862

Portrait of Mr. J. H. Corbett, 1831 (p.43)
oil on panel
29 7/8 x 24 3/8
Portland Museum of Art (1996 gift)

Portrait of Mrs. J. H. Corbett, 1831 (p.43)
oil on panel
29 15/16 x 24 5/16
Portland Museum of Art (1996 gift)

WALDO PEIRCE
United States, 1884-1970

Haircut in the Kitchen, 1965
oil on canvas
30 x 22
Portland Museum of Art

Working a Maine Farm, n.d.
oil on canvas
20 3/8 x 24 1/4
Farnsworth Art Museum (1996 gift)

ALLEN ERSKINE PHILBRICK
United States, 1879-1964

Main Street, Damariscotta, Maine, 1936
oil on canvas
30 x 40
Farnsworth Art Museum

ROBERT POLLIEN
United States, born 1960

Barnes Island, circa 1989-90
oil on linen
23 7/8 x 26
Farnsworth Art Museum (1996 gift)

FAIRFIELD PORTER
United States, 1907-1975

Beach Flowers No. 2, 1972
oil on canvas
24 1/4 x 20 1/8
Farnsworth Art Museum

Bear Island, 1966 (p.78)
oil on board
14 1/4 x 18 1/4
Farnsworth Art Museum

EDWARD POTTHAST
United States, 1857-1927

Maine Harbor Scene #1, circa 1920
oil on board
4 7/8 x 7 3/8
Portland Museum of Art

Maine Harbor Scene #2, circa 1920
oil on board
4 7/8 x 7 3/8
Portland Museum of Art

MAURICE BRAZIL PRENDERGAST
United States, 1859-1924

Group of Boats (Watching the Regatta), 1907 (p.66)
watercolor and graphite on paper
11 1/2 x 15 1/4
Portland Museum of Art

WILLIAM MATTHEW PRIOR
United States, 1806-1873

Portrait of Eliza Smith Sewall, 1838 (p.49)
oil on canvas
34 1/4 x 28 1/8
Portland Museum of Art (1994 gift)

Portrait of Joseph Sewall, Jr., 1838 (p.49)
oil on canvas
34 1/8 x 27 7/8
Portland Museum of Art (1994 gift)

EDWARD WILLIS REDFIELD
United States, 1869-1965

The Toymaker's Home (Monhegan Island, Maine), 1928 (p.55)
oil on canvas
26 1/8 x 32 1/4
Monhegan Museum

PAUL RICKERT
United States, born 1947

Fuel for the Coast, 1991
watercolor on paper
15 x 41 1/2
Maine Maritime Museum

SEVERIN ROESEN
United States (born Germany), 1814/15-1872

Still Life–Fruit on a Marble Table, circa 1855-1865
oil on panel
9 1/2 x 11 3/4
Portland Museum of Art (1993 gift)

KARL SCHRAG
United States, 1912-1995

The Green Night, 1982
oil on canvas
40 x 50
Farnsworth Art Museum (1996 gift)

FRANK HENRY SHAPLEIGH
United States, 1842-1906

Lovel's Pond from Jockey Cap, Fryeburg, Maine, circa 1872 (p.34)
oil on canvas
14 1/4 x 24 1/8
Portland Museum of Art (1996 gift)

LAURENCE SISSON
United States, born 1928

View of Stonington, early 1960s
watercolor on paper
20 1/2 x 29
Farnsworth Art Museum

HELENA WOOD SMITH
United States, active early 1900s

Matinicus, circa 1900
oil on canvasboard
4 3/4 x 8 1/2
Monhegan Museum

JOSEPH B. SMITH
United States, 1798-1876

The Richard Morse, circa 1852
oil on canvas
24 1/2 x 45 1/2
Maine Maritime Museum

HERMANN DUDLEY MURPHY
Zinnias and Marigolds

1932

oil on panel

16 x 12 in.

Portland Museum of Art

JOSEPH NICOLETTI
Night Still Life

1990

oil on canvas

50 x 40 in.

Portland Museum of Art

XANTHUS RUSSELL SMITH
United States, 1839-1929

Somes Sound, n.d.
oil on paper
7 1/2 x 11 1/8
Farnsworth Art Museum

Untitled, 1893 and 1910
watercolor and graphite on paper
6 5/8 x 9 11/16
Farnsworth Art Museum

ROBERT SOLOTAIRE
United States, born 1930

Dragon Cement II, 1995
oil on board
15 3/8 x 22
Farnsworth Art Museum (1996 gift)

RAPHAEL SOYER
United States, 1899-1987

The Boatyard, Vinalhaven, circa 1950
oil on canvas
16 1/8 x 20
Farnsworth Art Museum (1996 gift)

CARL SPRINCHORN
United States, 1887-1971

Cosmos, 1936
oil on board
17 7/8 x 24
Farnsworth Art Museum

Gloria October, Shin Pond, Maine, 1946 (p.71)
oil on canvas
26 x 34
Portland Museum of Art

HELEN ST. CLAIR
United States, born 1931

Sailmaker and Son II, n.d.
oil on canvas
16 3/4 x 20
Maine Maritime Museum

EDITH A. STERNFELD
United States, 1898-1990

Untitled (Boat Builders), n.d.
watercolor on paper
14 1/2 x 21 1/2
Maine Maritime Museum

ALICE KENT STODDARD
United States, 1885-1976

Mending the Nets, mid-20th century
oil on canvasboard
20 x 24
Monhegan Museum

DONALD STONE
United States, born 1929

Caulkers, circa 1984
watercolor on paper
21 x 21
Monhegan Museum

Christmas Cove, Monhegan, circa 1984
oil on masonite
24 x 38
Monhegan Museum

JOHN SWAN
United States, born 1948

Regatta, 1984
watercolor on paper
19 1/2 x 29 1/2
Portland Museum of Art

ALICE SWETT
United States, 1847-1916

Untitled (House on Monhegan Island), circa 1895-1900
watercolor on paper
4 3/4 x 4
Monhegan Museum

Untitled (House on Monhegan Island), circa 1895-1900
watercolor on paper
8 3/4 x 12
Monhegan Museum

REUBEN TAM
United States, 1916-1991

Headland #1, The Passage, circa 1970-1980
watercolor on paper
11 3/4 x 13 3/4
Monhegan Museum

North Rock Fall, 1979
oil on canvas
38 x 42
Monhegan Museum

JAMES TESCHNER
United States, born 1955

Untitled (Bucket on Post), 1978
oil on panel
20 x 15 7/8
Portland Museum of Art

WILLIAM THON
United States, born 1906

The Old Sloop, 1993
mixed media on paper
18 x 24
Farnsworth Art Museum

Working Sloop, circa 1984
watercolor on paper
19 3/16 x 26 3/8
Farnsworth Art Museum

SAMUEL P. R. TRISCOTT
England, 1846-1925

Monhegan from Manana, circa 1902-1912
watercolor on paper
13 x 19 3/16
Monhegan Museum

ROSS STERLING TURNER
United States, 1847-1915

Rose Rambler, 1907 (p.67)
oil on canvas
27 x 20 1/8
Portland Museum of Art

ABRAHAM WALKOWITZ
United States (born Russia), 1880-1965

Old Home, Ogunquit, Maine, 1926
oil on canvas
26 x 40 1/2
Portland Museum of Art

EDMUND WARD
United States, 1892-1990

Cleaning Fish, n.d.
oil on canvasboard
19 7/8 x 23 3/4
Monhegan Museum

GEORGE WASSON
United States, 1855-1926

Ships at Harbor, n.d.
oil on canvas
18 x 24
Maine Maritime Museum

FREDERICK JUDD WAUGH
United States, 1861-1940

Lifting Gale, n.d.
oil on masonite
25 1/8 x 30 1/8
Farnsworth Art Museum

White Surf, circa 1920
oil on board
30 x 39 7/8
Portland Museum of Art

NEIL WELLIVER
United States, born 1929

Prospect Ice Flow, 1976 (p.79)
acrylic on canvas
71 7/8 x 95 13/16
Farnsworth Art Museum

G. WHITEHEAD
Great Britain, active 1820s

Portrait of a Gentleman, 1827
watercolor and graphite on paper
12 3/8 x 9 1/2
Portland Museum of Art

Portrait of a Lady, 1827
watercolor and graphite on paper
12 3/8 x 9 1/2
Portland Museum of Art

WILLIAM WILSON
United States, 1884-after 1940

Port Clyde, n.d.
watercolor on paper
13 1/8 x 17 15/16
Farnsworth Art Museum

ANDREW WINTER
United States, 1892-1958

Below Zero - Two Lights, Cape Elizabeth, 1934
oil on canvas
22 1/8 x 28 1/4
Portland Museum of Art

The Mailboat, mid-20th century
oil on canvas
30 1/8 x 20 1/2
Monhegan Museum

FAIRFIELD PORTER
Bear Island

1966

oil on board

14 1/4 x 18 1/4 in.

Farnsworth Art Museum